Junior How to Draw
Wild Animals

Published by Top That! Publishing plc
Tide Mill Way, Woodbridge, Suffolk, IP12 1AP, UK
www.topthatpublishing.com
Copyright © 2011 Top That! Publishing plc
0246897531
Printed and bound in China

Introduction

Have you always wanted to draw lions, tigers, elephants and other wild animals, but were put off because they looked too difficult? Have no fear! This book shows you a fun and easy way to draw all kinds of wild animals!

Just follow the tips and step-by-step instructions, and you'll soon learn a set of basic drawing techniques that you can then apply to any subject.

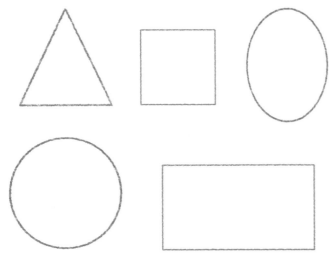

Basic Shapes

When you want to draw an object, a good way to start is to look at the object carefully and to break it down in your mind into a series of simple shapes — triangles, squares, rectangles, circles and ovals.

Top Tip!

To draw good, clear lines, you need to keep your pencils nice and sharp with a pencil sharpener.

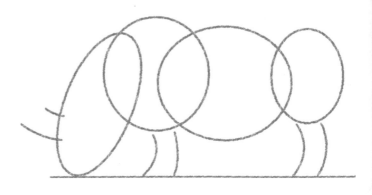

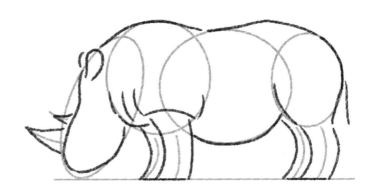

Animals tend to break down mostly into ovals and circles, with additional curved lines for arms, legs and tails.

Notice which shapes are bigger or smaller than others, and where they join together. Look carefully at their angles and proportions. Spend time just looking before you pick up your pencil!

Tools of the Trade

You will need a pencil, an eraser, a pencil sharpener, a ruler, a fine black marker pen and fibre-tip pens or pencils for colouring in your drawings.

Four Simple Steps

You can apply the 'basic shapes' technique to drawing any subject, including animals. You can use it for simple front-on and side-on views, as well as for more complicated angled views. All it takes is four simple steps ...

Step 1. First, break the animal down into its basic shapes.

Step 2. Next, sketch a simple outline using the shapes as guidelines.

Step 3. Build up the detail, then go over your pencil sketch in pen.

Step 4. Finally, add colour to bring your picture to life!

Drawing Faces Front-on

If you are drawing an animal's face front-on, both halves need to look the same. The best way to achieve this is to lightly sketch a cross on the face as a guide. Position the eyes on the horizontal line of the cross. The vertical line is called the 'line of symmetry', and the features should be exactly the same on both sides of this line.

Perspective

Many of the drawings in this book show animals seen from an angle. When you look at a drawing, it should be obvious where the artist was in relation to what was being drawn. This is known as 'perspective'.

The basic rule of perspective is that things in the distance appear smaller than those closer to the viewer.

Wildebeest

Your starting point for drawing a wildebeest is just two ovals and a few curved lines!

Side-on View

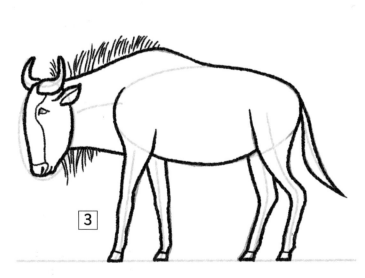

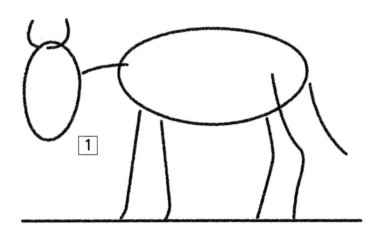

Step 1. For your outline of a wildebeest, start by drawing a large oval for the body and a smaller one for the head. Then add lines to show the position of the horns, neck, legs and tail, as shown.

Step 2. Next, lightly sketch in the wildebeest's thick neck, then its slender legs, curved horns and tail. Draw the outline shape of the head and add an ear. Finally, mark a dot to show the position of the eye.

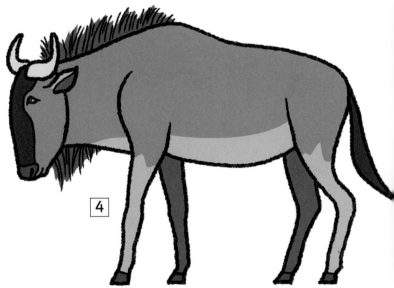

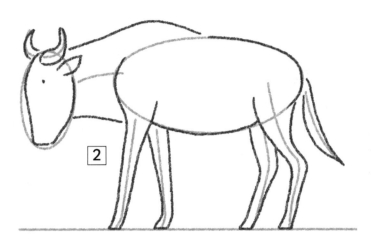

Step 3. Go over your pencil outline with a fine black marker pen. Next, draw in the eye, nose, muzzle and face markings, and add the mane using light strokes of the pen.

Step 4. Once you are happy with your outline, rub out any pencil guidelines. Then use fibre-tip pens or pencils to colour in your wildebeest. Give it a greyish-brown body and black face markings.

Bear

Now have a go at drawing this cute but dangerous grizzly bear!

Fact File

A well-known type of brown bear is the grizzly bear. It has a hump on its shoulders, long claws and very strong hind (back) legs.

Side-on View

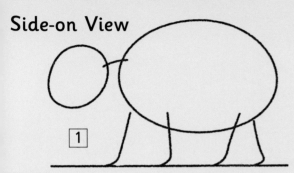

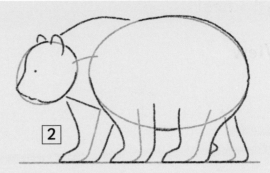

Step 1. Lightly sketch a large oval for the body, a smaller one for the head and five short lines for the neck and legs.

Step 2. Now draw the outline of the bear around your pencil guidelines. Look carefully at the shape of the face so that you get the nose right!

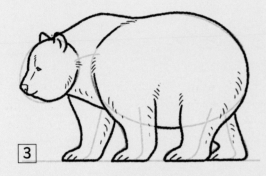

Step 3. Go over your pencil outline in black pen, leaving a gap on the right side of the cheek for fur. Add the nose, eye, mouth and toes, and then use short strokes to suggest fur on the face, legs and body.

Step 4. Colour in your bear, making the two far-side legs a darker shade to show they are in shadow.

Lizard

Using your new drawing skills, have a go at this view of a lively lizard!

Top Tip!

Take your time to carefully copy each step.

Side-on View

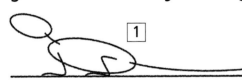

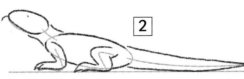

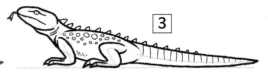

Step 1. Begin by sketching your guidelines, as shown above.

Step 2. Now draw the lizard's outline shape. Give it a thick neck and tail, bent legs and a tongue.

Step 3. Add details, such as the eye, mouth, forked tongue and body scales. Then go over your pencil lines in black pen.

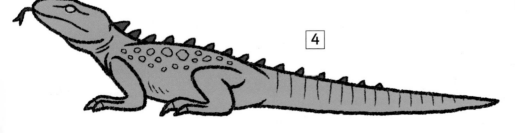

Step 4. Rub out the pencil guidelines and colour in your lizard. Don't be afraid to experiment with different colours and shading.

Elephant Walking

Have fun drawing this powerful African elephant – the largest animal on land.

Fact File

To keep healthy, elephants take a daily dust bath. Using their trunk, they spray dust over their skin. The dust acts as a sunscreen and insect repellent.

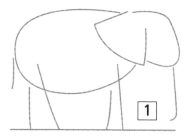

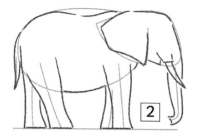

Step 1. Lightly sketch these guidelines. Try and match the angles of the legs.

Step 2. Now draw the elephant's outline around your guidelines. Notice the dip in the elephant's back, and the shape of the ear.

Step 3. Go over your outline in black pen and add some fine detail, such as the eye, toenails and wrinkles in the skin.

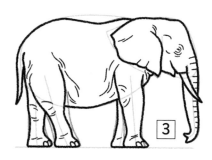

Side-on View

Step 4. Rub out any remaining pencil lines and colour your mighty African elephant grey.

Elephant Turning

The elephant has spotted you and is turning to look! This time, draw him approaching.

Top Tip!

To avoid smudges, try not to rest your hand on areas of your drawing that you are working on.

Angled View

Step 1. Sketch the elephant's shape, copying the angles of the legs and ears. Add a cross on the face as a position guide for the eyes.

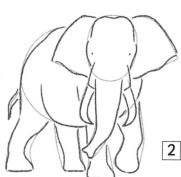

Step 2. Go over the outline shape, adjusting and curving it where necessary to make it more lifelike. Add two dots for eyes on the crossbar of the cross.

Step 3. Start to add finer detail, such as eyes, wrinkles and toenails. Then go over your sketch in black pen.

Step 4. Using a grey pen or pencil – or even charcoal if you've got some – colour in your magnificent elephant.

Rhino

Try these two views of a powerful rhino with its huge nose horns.

Rhino Side-on

1

Step 1. Overlap four ovals. Then add lines for the legs and horns.

2

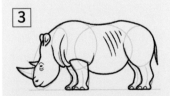

Step 2. Draw the shape of the rhino around the guidelines, and add some folds in the skin.

3

Step 3. Add further details, as shown, then go over your pencil outline in pen.

4

Step 4. Rub out the guidelines and colour in your African rhino.

Angled View

1

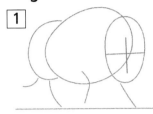

Step 1. Start by copying these guidelines. Include a cross on the face as a position guide for the facial features.

2

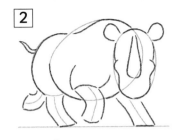

Step 2. Draw the rhino's outline around your guidelines. Include its horn, ears and tail.

3

Step 3. Build up the detail and go over your outline in black pen.

Step 4. Once you are happy with your drawing, rub out the guidelines and colour in your running rhino!

4

Hippo

Next, have a go at a hippo!

Angled View

1

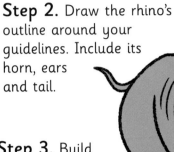

Step 1. Begin by lightly sketching the basic shape, as shown above.

2

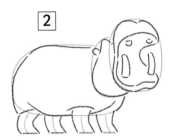

Step 2. Use your guideline shapes to help you draw the hippo's outline.

3

Step 3. Go over your sketch in pen, adding details such as whiskers, wrinkles and toenails.

4

Step 4. Rub out the guidelines and colour in your yawning hippo!

Top Tip!

You can always add a background to your pictures. Start with basic shapes, then build up the detail.

Tiger Prowling

The stunning stripes on this prowling tiger make it great fun to draw!

Side-on View

Fact File

The tiger is the largest and rarest member of the cat family. In the wild it usually lives alone, and has a lifespan of about 15 years.

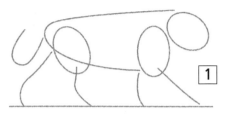

Step 1. Sketch three ovals and connect them with a loop. Next, draw lines to show the position of the legs and tail.

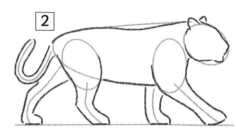

Step 2. Draw the outline of the tiger with its strong shoulders, represented by the centre oval.

Step 3. Fill in the details of the face. Then start to add the stunning stripes. Go over your drawing in black pen.

Step 4. Rub out the pencil guidelines and have fun colouring in your tiger.

Tiger Leaping

Scare your friends by drawing this fearsome tiger at the moment of attack!

Angled View

Step 1. Lightly sketch three overlapping ovals and carefully position the lines for the legs and tail. Include a cross on the face as a position guide.

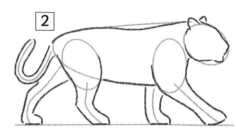

Step 2. Draw the tiger's outline around your guidelines, then sketch in the eyes, nose and mouth using the cross as a guide. Make the front paws bigger than the back ones because they are nearer to you.

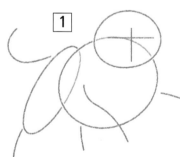

Step 3. Work up the detail on the face. Then draw in the stripes, which bend around the body. Go over your pencil sketch in black pen.

Step 4. Rub out the pencil guidelines and give the tiger its bold camouflage!

Lion

Have fun drawing two views of the magnificent 'king of the jungle'!

Lion Front-on

Step 1. Sketch three ovals and a cross, plus lines for the body and feet, as shown above.

Step 2. Sketch the lion's outline, and use the cross to position the facial features.

Step 3. Go over your outline in black pen and build up the fine detail.

Step 4. Rub out the pencil guidelines and colour your lion in shades of brown.

Side-on View

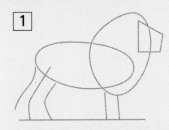

Step 1. First, sketch the guidelines for your picture, as shown above.

Step 2. Draw the lion's outline shape around your guidelines.

Step 3. Go over your sketch in black pen and add fine detail to the face, mane and feet.

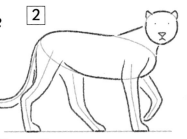

Step 4. Rub out the pencil guidelines and colour in your noble lion.

Cheetah

This cheetah has spotted you! Can you draw him before he sprints away?

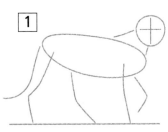

Step 1. The guidelines include a sloping body shape, a small circle for the head with a cross, a thick neck and longer back legs.

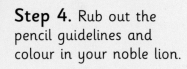

Step 2. Draw the cheetah's outline and mark the eyes, nose and mouth, using the cross as a position guide.

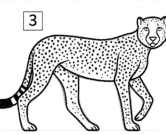

Step 3. Go over your pencil outline in black pen and start to add the body markings.

Step 4. Rub out the pencil guidelines and colour in your speedy cheetah.

Zebra

Have fun drawing this stripy character. Take time to get the stripes just right!

Fact File
Each zebra has its own unique pattern of stripes that breaks up its outline in the grass, especially at dawn when predators are about!

Side-on View

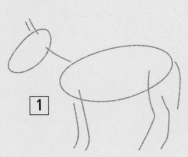

1

2

Step 2. Next, draw your zebra's outline around the guidelines. Carefully shape the head and add a guideline for the mane.

3

Step 1. First, create your guidelines by sketching two ovals for the body and head, and then lines to represent the legs, tail, neck and ears.

4

Step 3. Draw in the eye, nose and mouth. Next, go over your pencil outline in black pen. Then start to add the stripy markings.

Step 4. Make sure the stripes vary in thickness – they should taper at the ends to make it look as if they are curving around the zebra's body. Now colour it in!

Horse

In the wild, horses often rear up in play. They may also rear if frightened or to threaten another animal.

Angled View

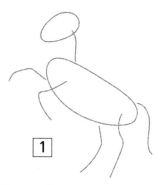

1

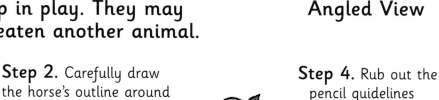

2

Step 2. Carefully draw the horse's outline around your guidelines. Shape the head inside the oval and add a mane and tail.

Step 4. Rub out the pencil guidelines and colour in your beautiful horse.

4

Step 1. Sketch the body and head shapes, taking care to get the right distance between them. Then add lines for the neck, legs and tail.

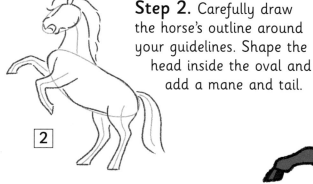

3

Step 3. Go back over your outline, making sure you have got the curves just right, especially on the legs. Add details such as the eye, cheek, nose, mouth and hooves. Then go over it again in pen.

Giraffe

Giraffes are fun to draw because they have such a long neck and legs!

Fact File

The giraffe is the tallest animal on Earth. Like zebras, no two giraffes have the same pattern!

Side-on View

1

Step 1. First, draw a small oval for the head, then a long line for the neck. Draw a larger oval for the body and add four guidelines for the legs and one for the tail.

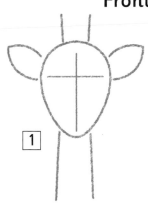

2

Step 2. Next, draw the giraffe's outline. Notice where the neck joins the body, and give the neck a bulge for the shoulders. Carefully shape the face inside the smaller oval.

3

Step 3. Add the giraffe's face and bold markings, and then go over your pencil lines in black pen.

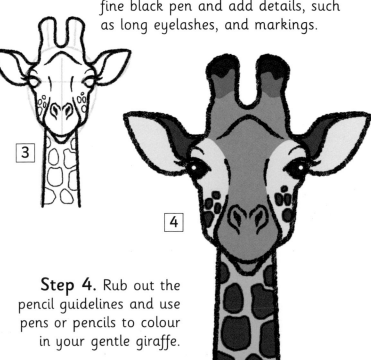

4

Step 4. Finally, rub out the pencil guidelines and colour in your very tall friend.

Giraffe's Head

This detailed drawing lets you practise symmetry – getting both halves the same.

Front-on View

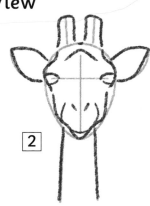

1

Step 1. First, sketch the outline shown above. Use a ruler to draw the cross in the middle of the face.

2

Step 2. Refine the shape of the face and ears and draw in the horns. Then, using the cross as a guide, add the eyes, nose and mouth. Make sure both halves are the same!

Step 3. Go over your pencil marks in fine black pen and add details, such as long eyelashes, and markings.

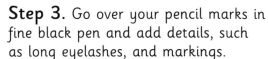

3

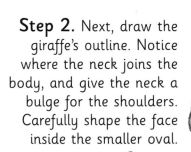

4

Step 4. Rub out the pencil guidelines and use pens or pencils to colour in your gentle giraffe.

11

Water Buffalo

Try your hand at these hefty water buffalo.

Fact File

Water buffalo spend most of their day submerged in muddy water eating grass and reeds.

Angled View

Step 1. For the angled view, lightly sketch the guidelines as shown above.

Step 2. Next, draw the animal's outline shape.

Step 3. Refine the shape and add further detail. Then go over your outline in pen.

Step 4. Rub out the pencil guidelines and colour in using various shades of grey.

Side-on View

Step 1. First, lightly sketch the basic shapes. Give your water buffalo a large body and a thick neck.

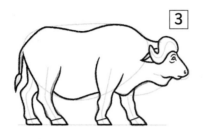

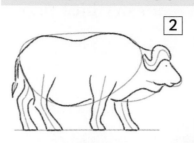

Step 2. Draw the water buffalo's outline, paying attention to all its curves, and begin to add detail.

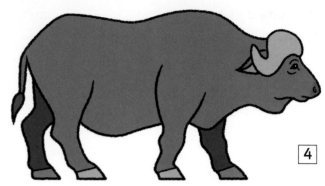

Step 3. Go over your outline in black pen and work up the finer detail.

Step 4. Rub out the guidelines and colour your water buffalo grey.

Impala

A leaping impala makes a great action picture!

Step 1. First, copy these guidelines, paying particular attention to the angle of the neck and shape of the legs.

Step 2. Next, draw the impala's outline around your guidelines and mark a dot for the eye.

Step 3. Add detail to the face, horns and hooves, and go over your outline in fine black pen.

Top Tip!

Take a look at wildlife documentaries to get a sense of what the animals are like in real life!

Side-on View

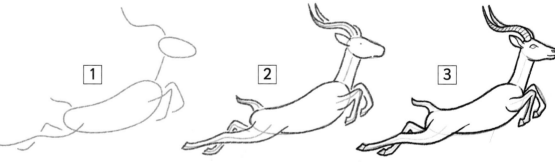

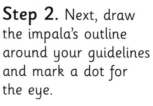

Step 4. Rub out any pencil lines and colour in your amazing antelope.

Crocodile Side-on

Here's a scaly croc to get your teeth into – but watch he doesn't bite first!

Fact File
Crocodiles lurk like floating logs in rivers and lakes, and leap out of the water to catch their prey.

Step 1. First, sketch a long oval for the body and a smaller one for the head. Then draw lines to show the position of the neck, legs and tail.

Step 2. Draw the croc's outline shape around your guidelines and give him an eye, mouth and claws.

Step 3. Next, add detail to the face and draw scales on the body, legs and tail. Go over your outline in black pen.

Step 4. Rub out the pencil guidelines and colour in your croc. Experiment with different shades of green for a varied effect.

Crocodile Angled View

Now you know how to draw a side-on croc, see if you can do him from a snappy angle!

Step 1. Start by sketching a large oval. Then overlap two smaller ones for the jaws. Add lines for the legs and tail.

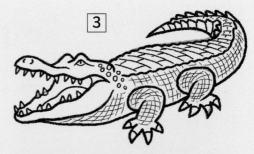

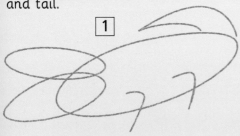

Step 2. Draw the croc's outline, taking care to position the head and jaws inside the two smaller ovals.

Step 3. Add the crocodile's eye, nostrils and teeth. Then start to carefully draw in the scales. Go over your work in fine black pen.

Step 4. Finally, rub out the pencil guidelines and bring your croc to life by adding colour.

Chameleon

Some chameleons can change colour! Why not make yours eye-catching?

Fact File

Chameleons are inquisitive, colourful lizards that live in warm habitats, such as rainforests.

Side-on View

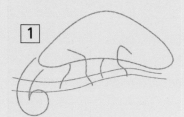

Step 1. Start by sketching the body shape, then add guidelines for the legs and tail, and a branch.

Step 2. Use the guidelines to help you draw the chameleon's outline and face.

Step 3. Go over your outline in black pen and add the markings.

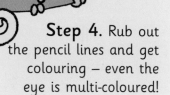

Step 4. Rub out the pencil lines and get colouring – even the eye is multi-coloured!

Angled View

Step 1. Sketch your guidelines, starting with the head.

Step 3. Go over your pencil outline in black pen and add details and markings.

Step 2. Draw the outline and face. Notice how the feet grip the branch.

Step 4. Rub out any pencil lines and have fun colouring in your chameleon!

Snake

You'll get plenty of practice drawing curves with this slithering snake!

Step 1. Draw two lines for the branch. Then draw an oval for the head and three large U-shapes for the lower body. Next, sketch the long curve of the upper body.

Step 4. Colour in, leaving highlighted areas white to suggest the snake is shiny.

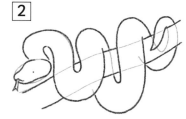

Step 2. Shape the head a little, and rub out the two sections of the snake's body that pass behind the branch.

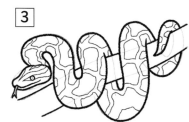

Step 3. Go over your outline in black pen, add detail to the face and draw the snake's markings.

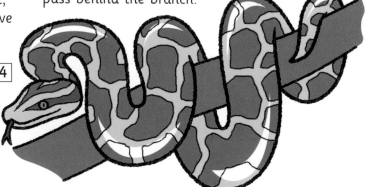

Gorilla
Try tackling this great ape from the side and then from an angle.

Fact File
Gorillas are the largest apes. When angry or excited, the males stand upright on their legs and pound their chest with their hands.

Side-on View

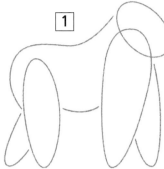

Step 1. First, sketch a slanting oval for the head, then draw the guidelines for the legs and link up with lines for the back and tummy.

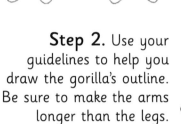

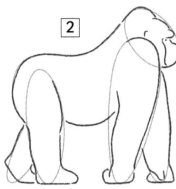

Step 2. Use your guidelines to help you draw the gorilla's outline. Be sure to make the arms longer than the legs.

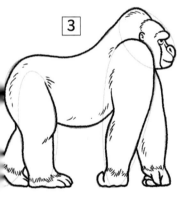

Step 3. Go over your outline in black pen and add detail to the face, hands and feet. Use short pen-strokes to suggest fur.

Step 4. Rub out the pencil guidelines and colour in your gentle giant.

Angled View

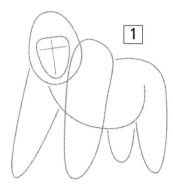

Step 1. Starting with the head, lightly sketch the guidelines shown here. Use a ruler to draw a cross on the face.

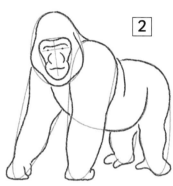

Step 2. Next, draw your gorilla's outline with its large, domed head and big shoulders. Then, using the cross as a guide, add the eyes, nose and mouth.

Step 3. Once you are happy with your sketch, go over your outline in black pen. Add fur and toes, as well as fine detail to the face.

Step 4. Rub out any remaining pencil lines and colour in. Gorillas have dark brown eyes, and adult males have a saddle-shaped patch of silver fur on their broad back.

Baboon

This large monkey can be fierce and noisy. First try a side-on view, then an angled one.

Fact File

Baboons live in groups, called troops. The troop may include anything from five to 250 animals.

Step 1. First, create your guidelines. Start with a small oval for the head and overlap with a large oval for the body. Add lines for the neck, legs, feet and tail.

Side-on View

Step 2. Use the guidelines to help you draw the baboon's outline. Give the head a brow ridge over the eyes and a distinct cheek pouch.

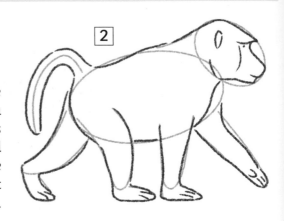

Step 4. Bring your baboon to life by colouring him in!

Step 3. Add the nose marking, then go over your pencil outline in black pen. Use long and short lines to suggest fur.

Angled View

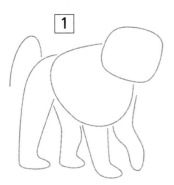

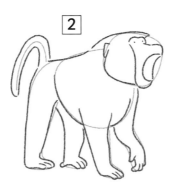

Step 4. Rub out the pencil lines and colour your fierce baboon a brownish-grey.

Step 1. For this angled view, start with an almost square shape for the head. Then complete the guidelines, as shown above.

Step 2. Sketch the baboon's outline, carefully shaping the head and feet. Draw in the eyes, open mouth and toes.

Step 3. Add detail, concentrating on the face. Then go over your outline in black pen. Use long and short strokes to suggest fur.

Orangutan

Can you get to grips with this lovable orangutan swinging and walking along?

Fact File
Orangutans are intelligent apes. They use sticks to spear fish and to get at the pulpy part of prickly fruit, and they use leaves as umbrellas!

Side-on View

1
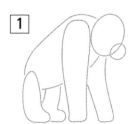

Step 1. Begin by sketching your orangutan guidelines.

2
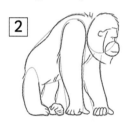

Step 2. Next, draw the ape's outline, with its short legs and long arms.

3

Step 3. Build up the detail, then go over your sketch in black pen. Add wavy strokes for fur.

4

Step 4. Rub out the pencil guidelines and colour in using shades of orange and grey.

Front-on View

1
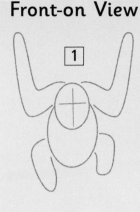

Step 1. Create your guidelines, as shown, and draw a cross on the face.

2

Step 2. Draw the outline, taking care with the hands and feet. Use the cross to position the eyes.

3
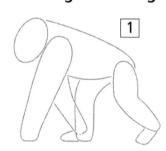

Step 3. Work up the fine detail and go over your sketch in black pen.

4

Step 4. Rub out any pencil lines and colour in using light and dark shades.

Chimpanzee

Now try drawing this cheeky chimpanzee!

1
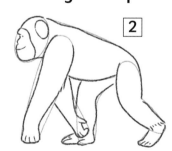

Step 1. Start by sketching an oval for the head. Then complete the guidelines as shown.

2

Step 2. Next, draw the chimp's outline, using the guidelines to get the angles right.

Step 4. Rub out the guidelines and colour in your cheeky chimp. Make the far-side arm and leg a darker shade to show they are in shadow.

3

Step 3. Use a black pen to go over your outline and add further detail.

Kangaroo Hopping

A hopping kangaroo uses its tail to help it balance. Can you capture its likeness?

Step 1. Sketch a small oval for the head and a larger one for the body. Add lines for the ears, neck, arms, legs and long tail.

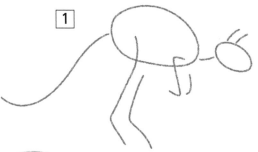

Step 2. Next, draw the kangaroo's outline. Keep the tail thick all the way to the tip.

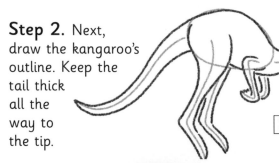

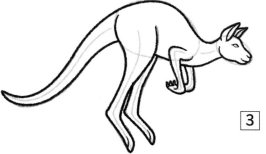

Step 3. Draw the face, ears and feet in more detail, then go over your outline in black pen.

Step 4. Rub out any pencil lines and colour in your bouncy kangaroo.

Kangaroo Standing

This kangaroo has a baby joey peeping out – good practice for drawing heads!

Step 1. Sketch your guidelines in pencil, as shown here.

Step 3. Build up the detail on the faces and feet, and add a few lines for skin folds. Then go over your outline in black pen.

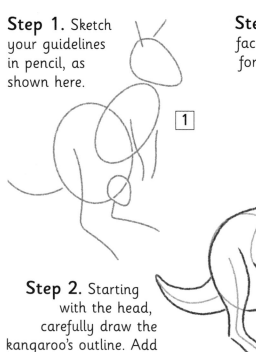

Step 2. Starting with the head, carefully draw the kangaroo's outline. Add a dot for the eye.

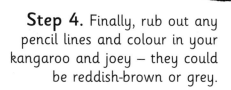

Step 4. Finally, rub out any pencil lines and colour in your kangaroo and joey – they could be reddish-brown or grey.

Koala

Try drawing this cuddly-looking koala!

Front-on View

Fact File
Koalas spend much of their time munching almost exclusively on eucalyptus leaves.

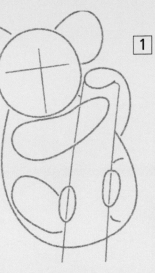

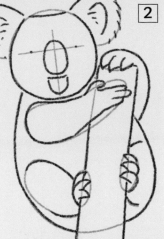

Step 1. Start by drawing a circle for the face – use a ruler to put a cross in it. Next, draw the ears, then the body shape. Add the branch, followed by the arms, legs and feet.

Step 2. Flatten the top of the head. Then, using the cross as a guide, mark two dots for eyes and draw the nose and mouth. Use short dashes to make the ears look furry. Next, complete the koala's outline, taking care with the fingers and toes.

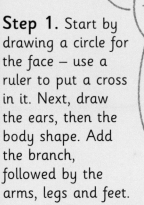

Step 3. Add further detail, such as eyebrows, nostrils, toenails and fur, then go over your pencil lines with black pen.

Step 4. Finally, rub out any pencil guidelines and colour in your cheerful koala.

Wombat

The stocky wombat uses its strong front claws for digging burrows.

Step 4. Rub out the guidelines and colour in your furry friend.

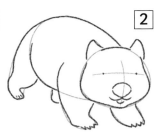

Step 1. Start with a circle and cross for the face, then add the ears, body and legs.

Step 2. Draw the outline and add two dots on the cross for eyes, a large nose and a mouth.

Step 3. Add further detail, then go over your outline in black pen.

Ostrich Running

Have fun drawing the lanky legs of this running ostrich.

Fact File
Ostriches are the largest bird on Earth. They stand at about 2.6 m (8.5 ft) tall. Unable to fly, they escape predators by running as fast as 45 mph.

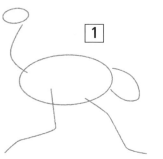

Step 4. Rub out any remaining pencil lines and colour in your ostrich.

Step 1. Sketch your guidelines, starting with the head. Be careful to get the angles of the neck and legs right.

Step 2. Shape the head and complete the rest of the outline. Use V-shaped strokes for the edges of the wings.

Step 3. Add more detail and use short dashes to suggest feathers. Go over your pencil sketch in pen.

Ostrich Standing

Front-on, the inquisitive ostrich looks quite comical!

Top Tip!
Don't throw away any of your drawings! Date them, and keep them in a portfolio. This is a great way to record your progress over time.

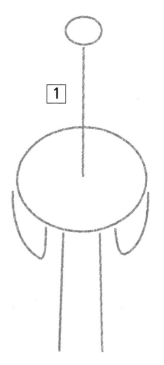

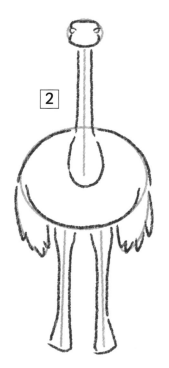

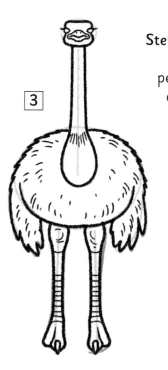

Step 4. To finish, rub out any pencil lines and colour in your gangling bird!

Step 1. Draw your guideline shapes, starting with a small oval for the head. Keep the neck and legs the same length.

Step 2. Shape the head and complete the ostrich's outline. Make the base of the neck slightly wider than the head.

Step 3. Draw the eyes, eyelashes, beak, big knees and other details. Then go over your outline in black pen.

Parrot Perching

Parrots use their long claws to grip the branches of their treetop perches.

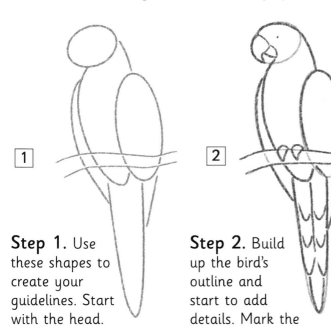

1

2

Step 1. Use these shapes to create your guidelines. Start with the head.

Step 2. Build up the bird's outline and start to add details. Mark the position of the eye.

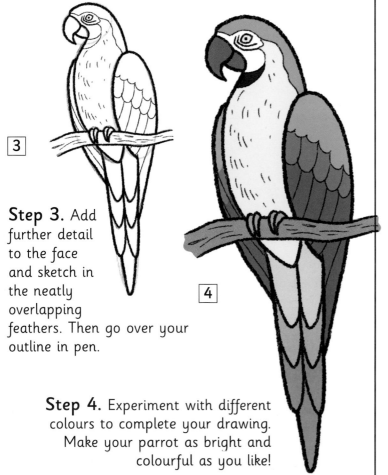

3

4

Step 3. Add further detail to the face and sketch in the neatly overlapping feathers. Then go over your outline in pen.

Step 4. Experiment with different colours to complete your drawing. Make your parrot as bright and colourful as you like!

Fact File
Many species of parrot can copy human speech and sounds!

Parrot Flying

Have fun drawing the parrot's wings!

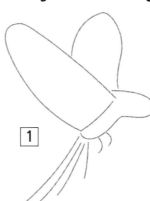

1

2

3

Step 1. Create a basic outline by sketching these simple shapes.

Step 2. Build up your basic outline by carefully shaping the head, wings, feet and tail-feathers.

Step 3. Add wrinkles around the eye, markings, and two rows of feathers on the wings. Then go over your outline in black pen.

Step 4. Rub out any remaining pencil lines and colour in your beautiful parrot. Have fun choosing bright colours!

4

Pelican

Have a go at two views of a pelican

Fact File

Pelicans have a long bill and large throat pouch, which they use to scoop up fish from the sea.

Pelican Side-on

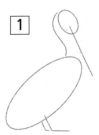

Step 1. Sketch two ovals, then add lines for the beak, neck, legs and feet.

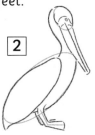

Step 2. Use your guidelines to help draw the bird's outline.

Step 3. Add detail before going over your outline in pen.

Step 4. Rub out any pencil lines and colour in your pelican.

In Flight

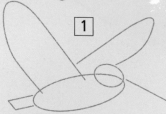

Step 1. Sketch two overlapping ovals for the head and body, then complete your guidelines as shown.

Step 2. Draw the pelican's outline and include its eye.

Step 3. Build up the detail, concentrating on the wing feathers. Then go over your outline sketch in black pen.

Step 4. Rub out the pencil guidelines and colour in your brown pelican.

Penguin

Draw a penguin in four simple steps!

Step 1. Lightly sketch four ovals and three lines to create the basic shape of your penguin.

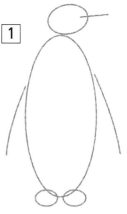

Step 2. Next, build up the penguin's outline around your guidelines.

Step 3. Add a little more detail to the face and feet. Then go over your outline in black pen.

Step 4. Rub out the pencil guidelines and colour in your majestic emperor penguin.

Bald Eagle

Amaze your friends by drawing two views of this magnificent bird of prey!

Fact File

The bald eagle is the national bird of the United States. It feeds mainly on fish, which it catches with its sharp claws.

Eagle Side-on

[1]

Step 1. Starting with the head, copy the guidelines above.

[2]

Step 2. Carefully draw the bird's outline around your guidelines.

[3]

Step 3. Draw in the feathers and other details. Then go over your sketch in pen.

[4]

Step 4. Rub out the guidelines and colour in your bald eagle.

In Flight

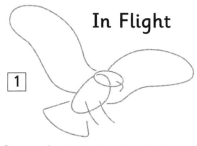

[1]

Step 1. Lightly sketch the guidelines shown above.

[3]

Step 3. Build up the detail, adding the feathers in neat rows. Then go over your outline in pen.

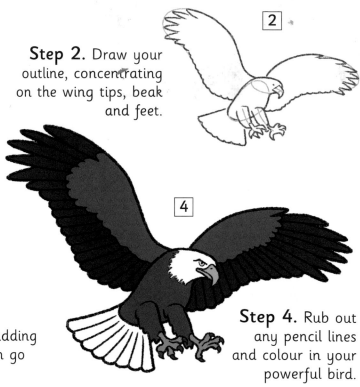

[2]

Step 2. Draw your outline, concentrating on the wing tips, beak and feet.

[4]

Step 4. Rub out any pencil lines and colour in your powerful bird.

Albatross

The albatross is one of the largest flying birds.

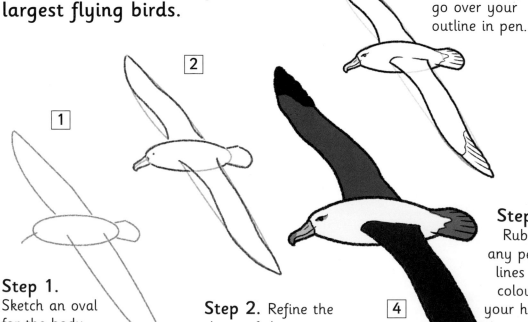

[1]

Step 1.
Sketch an oval for the body. Add a line for the beak, plus wings and a tail.

[2]

Step 2. Refine the shape of the wings and beak, and add a dot to mark the position of the eye.

[3]

Step 3. Add further detail and go over your outline in pen.

[4]

Step 4. Rub out any pencil lines and colour in your huge, soaring bird.

Conclusion
The more you practise, the easier your drawing will become.

Now that you have drawn all of the pictures in this book, why not have a go at doing some stunning drawings of your own?

Choose an animal and spend time looking at it before you begin. Try to see it in your mind as a series of basic shapes. Study its proportions and angles.

Perhaps the most important thing to remember is to always draw what you can actually see, not what you think something looks like!

Now take out your sketch pad, pencils, a sharpener, an eraser and a pen – **and get drawing!**

Drawing Cartoons
You can have great fun using your new drawing skills to create cartoon animals!

The technique is the same as when drawing realistic animals, except that now you can have fun exaggerating body parts and giving your animal cartoon features.

Step 1. Sketch an oval for your cartoon croc's body and two large overlapping shapes for the head. Add the tail and two lines as guides for the position of the legs.

Step 2. Next, draw your cartoon croc's outline. Make the head almost as large as the body, and exaggerate the size of the eyes and the bumps on the end of its snout. Shape the open mouth into a cheeky smile.

Step 4. Finally, rub out any pencil guidelines and colour in your snappy cartoon crocodile.

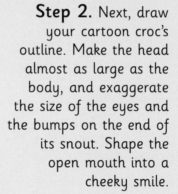

Step 3. Have fun distorting your cartoon croc's features. Give it large eyes, nostrils and teeth, and add a dimple at the corner of the mouth. Work up the detail and go over your outline in pen.